AUG -- 2020
Stark County District Library
www.StarkLibrary.org
330.452.0665

Cats
Scottish Fold Cats

Leo Statts

abdobooks.com

Published by Abdo Zoom, a division of ABDO, PO Box 398166, Minneapolis, Minnesota 55439. Copyright © 2020 by Abdo Consulting Group, Inc. International copyrights reserved in all countries. No part of this book may be reproduced in any form without written permission from the publisher. Launch!™ is a trademark and logo of Abdo Zoom.

Printed in the United States of America, North Mankato, Minnesota.

052019
092019

Photo Credits: iStock, Shutterstock

Production Contributors: Kenny Abdo, Jennie Forsberg, Grace Hansen, John Hansen

Design Contributors: Dorothy Toth, Neil Klinepier

Library of Congress Control Number: 2018963143

Publisher's Cataloging-in-Publication Data

Names: Statts, Leo, author.

Title: Scottish fold cats / by Leo Statts.

Description: Minneapolis, Minnesota : Abdo Zoom, 2020 | Series: Cats | Includes online resources and index.

Identifiers: ISBN 9781532127137 (lib. bdg.) | ISBN 9781532128110 (ebook) | ISBN 9781532128608 (Read-to-me ebook)

Subjects: LCSH: Scottish fold cat--Juvenile literature. | Cat, Domestic--Juvenile literature. | Cats--Behavior--Juvenile literature. | Cat breeds--Juvenile literature.

Classification: DDC 636.8--dc23

Table of Contents

Scottish Fold Cats........................4

Body...................................6

Care.................................10

Personality..........................14

History..............................18

Quick Stats..........................20

Glossary.............................22

Online Resources.....................23

Index................................24

Scottish Fold Cats

Scottish fold cats make great family pets. They like most people and other cats.

They even like dogs.

Body

A Scottish fold is not born with folded ears. A kitten's ears fold when it is about 21 days old.

Scottish folds have round faces.

They have round eyes, too.

Care

Scottish folds need scratching posts.

It is important to give Scottish folds toys to play with.

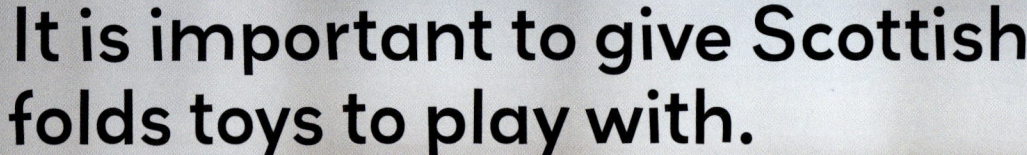

Scottish folds need a clean litter box, too.

Personality

Scottish folds are known to lay and sit in unusual **positions**. They often sleep on their backs with their legs sticking up.

Scottish folds do not like to be left alone. They enjoy the **company** of others.

History

The first known Scottish fold was born in 1961. She had ears that were folded down and forward.

A **shepherd** first saw the cat on a farm in Scotland.

19

Average Weight

A male Scottish fold weighs as much as a bowling ball.

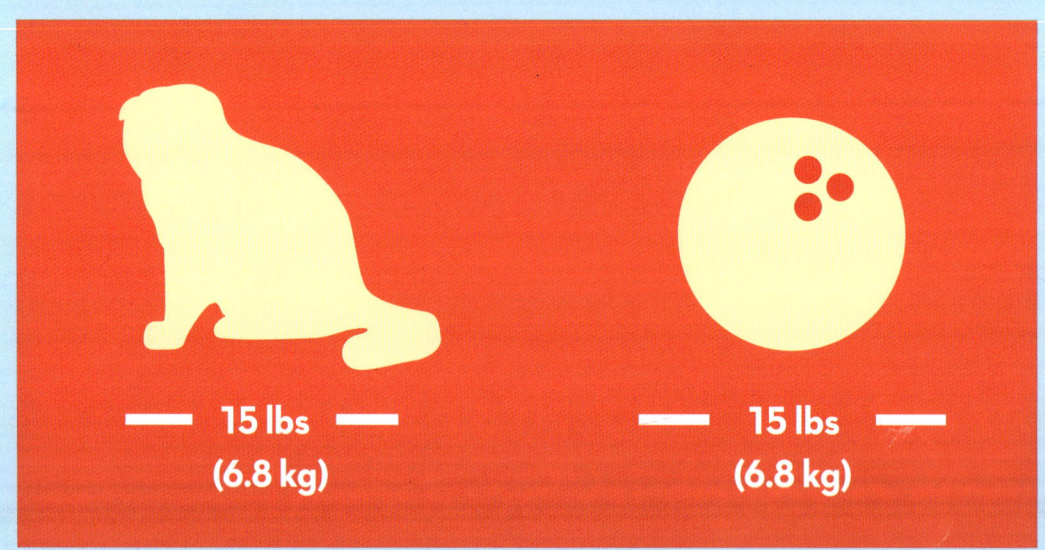

Average Weight

A female Scottish fold weighs less than a bowling ball.

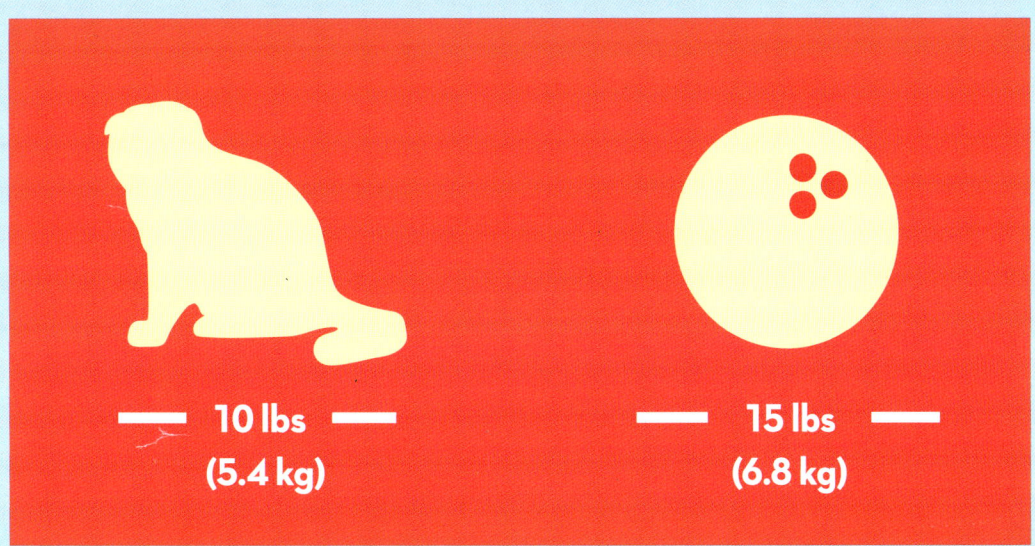

Glossary

company – being with another or others.

natural – having a certain need to do something by nature.

position – a certain way that a cat is sits or lays.

shepherd – a person who takes care of sheep.

Online Resources

For more information on Scottish fold cats, please visit **abdobooklinks.com** or scan this QR code.

Learn even more with the Abdo Zoom Animals database. Visit **abdozoom.com** today!

23

Index

dogs 5

ears 6, 18

eyes 9

face 8

head 6, 8, 9

legs 14

needs 10, 11, 12, 13, 16

personality 4, 5, 14, 16

Scotland 19

toys 12